THE MICKEY MOUSE WATCH

From the Beginning of Time

by Robert Heide
& John Gilman

A Welcome Book

HYPERION

NEW YORK

CONTENTS

PAGE 1: *Cartoon from* Mickey Mouse Annual, *Dean & Son, Ltd., London, 1943.*

PAGE 2: *Mickey Mouse lapel pocket watch with original cord, button and box.*

PAGE 3: *Mickey Mouse pocket watch with leather strap and round, metal fob.*

BELOW: *Big Bad Wolf alarm clock and box.*

Rare Ingersoll Mickey Mouse gold DeLuxe wristwatch in clear celluloid slip cover, 1939.

THE MICKEY MOUSE WATCH

The Mickey Mouse watch—particularly the original 1933 Ingersoll edition—has become an icon as identifiable and familiar as time itself. There is no simple answer as to why Mickey Mouse watches are so much more popular—and collectible—than watches featuring other comic book or cartoon characters. In any case, a Mickey Mouse watch—new or old—continues to be in great demand.

Tim Luke, the head of Christie's collectibles department in New York and a leading auctioneer and lecturer in the collectibles field, has said that the original Ingersoll Mickey Mouse wristwatches (and the attendant pocket watches and clocks) are pivotal and central to the theme of all Disneyana collecting.

This book is meant to be a history and chronological account (by decade) of Mickey Mouse watches of the 1930s, 1940s, 1950s, 1960s, 1970s, and the latter-day 1980s and 1990s limited edition/limited quantity watches. We've also highlighted other key Disney character watches that have become prized collectibles in the marketplace.

OPPOSITE:
1934 Ingersoll Mickey Mouse wristwatch with leather band, inside original box.

A vast quantity of Mickey Mouse watches—many of which were produced in limited numbers—were created during the 1980s and the 1990s by a variety of companies. New character watches are introduced often, sell out quickly, and turn up in the collectibles market at increased prices. Watches featuring Winnie the Pooh, the Dalmatians, and characters from *The Lion King*, *Toy Story*, and *The Hunchback of Notre Dame* abound. But our main focus is Mickey Mouse.

1936 Sears Roebuck catalog advertisement for Mickey Mouse timepieces.

We've created this book to be used primarily as a reference guide to what exists in the collectibles marketplace as well as in the new instant collectible and wearables arenas. This is not a complete encyclopedia since, after 1972, the watches are too numerous to create a full listing.

This study of the Mickey Mouse watch has been a great adventure into a special area of Disney history and American popular culture. We hope you will have as much of a sense of joy in the discovery of these watches as we have. It has really been FUN TIME with Mickey!

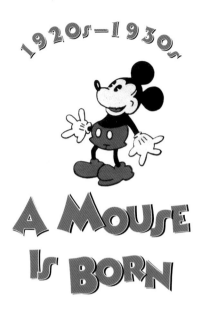

1920s–1930s

A Mouse Is Born

Steamboat *Willie* marked the public debut of Mickey Mouse. The first synchronized sound cartoon, the short premiered on November 18, 1928 (a date now regarded as Mickey Mouse's birthday) at the Colony Theater in New York. The public cheered—a new star was born.

OPPOSITE: *First Mickey Mouse Merchandise catalog from Kay Kamen Inc., New York, 1934.*

Pantages theater marquee in Hollywood highlights Tallulah Bankhead in Tarnished Lady and a Mickey Mouse comedy.

Two earlier silent shorts, *Plane Crazy* and *The Gallopin' Gaucho*, were subsequently released with sound added. No one was more amazed than Walt himself, who saw Mickey go on to star in 15 cartoons during 1928 and 1929. Mickey Mouse not only survived the stock market crash of 1929, his popularity remained in high gear during the years of the Great Depression. The success of the Mickey cartoons allowed Walt to build a large new Hollywood studio on Hyperion Avenue where he often repeated the now-famous line:

Walt Disney in 1932 with his cartoon creation: Mickey Mouse.

"I hope we never lose sight of one fact . . . that this was all started by a mouse."

A Merchant Mouse

During a visit to New York, soon after the October 29, 1929 Wall Street collapse, Walt Disney was followed by a mysterious man who cornered him in his hotel lobby and asked if Disney would allow him to put an image of Mickey Mouse on a school note tablet. At first Walt resisted the idea, but finally agreed to a deal that would pay him $300 in cash. This first Mickey Mouse writing tablet features a drawing of a smiling Mickey Mouse sitting at a school desk, reading a history book and holding an apple for his teacher. On the bright red, white, and black cover in bold letters is the name Mickey Mouse. In small letters at the bottom of the tablet is © 1930 Walter E. Disney. Thus the first bona fide piece of Mickey Mouse merchandise was created.

Mickey Mouse school tablet—the first time Mickey was used on a licensed product, 1930.

EARLY MICKEY PRODUCTS

Among the earliest merchandising successes for Mickey Mouse and his girlfriend Minnie were the Charlotte Clark stuffed dolls sold at Bullock's and The May Company in Los Angeles for $5. Soon enterprising seamstresses copied these dolls, and sold them at significantly lower prices to individuals and local stores that could not afford Disney's Charlotte Clark dolls' wholesale price of $30 per dozen.

Steamboat Willie *Mickey Mouse doll made by Charlotte Clark, early 1930s.*

The George Borgfeldt Company of New York signed a merchandising deal with Walt Disney Enterprises in 1930, and among its first products were Mickey Mouse handkerchiefs. Borgfeldt also produced and distributed a wood-jointed Mickey Mouse doll as well as an array of Mickey and Minnie hand-painted bisque figurines and toothbrush holders that were made in Japan.

RIGHT:
Hand-painted Mickey Mouse 1930s bisque figurine. Mickey's right arm is movable; his left arm and the cleft in his left shoe were designed to hold a toothbrush.

14

MICKEY MOUSE MERCHANDISE

To handle the many requests from various businesses to put Mickey Mouse on their products, Disney hired a full-time manager and promotional salesperson. Herman "Kay" Kamen, a former boys' outfitter, hat salesman and promoter of Our Gang products, signed an exclusive contract appointing him sole merchandise licensing representative for Walt Disney Enterprises. Prestigious firms were all too happy to license Mickey Mouse, gladly paying Disney royalties of 2½% to 10%.

Under Kay Kamen's leadership, sales of Mickey Mouse merchandise soared to several million dollars in 1933. Mickey Mouse could be found on a chocolate bar, soda pop, cookies, toothpaste, and his image was used in major campaigns to promote the sales of bread, milk, ice cream and Post Toasties breakfast cereals. A 1935 poster displayed in grocery stores proclaimed Mickey Mouse to be "the world's greatest salesman who rang up sales in 1934 to the tune of $35 million."

1935 Mickey Mouse Merchandise catalog cover, published by Kay Kamen, Inc.

The Comic Character Watch Parade

Harold Gray's Little Orphan Annie—one of America's favorite comic strip characters in the Depression era—was also popular on a radio show sponsored by Ovaltine, first heard over the Blue Network in 1931. Orphan Annie Ovaltine Beettleware shake-up mugs were found in most homes in those days; and in 1933 the New Haven Watch Company advertised a Little Orphan Annie wristwatch. By the time it was marketed early in 1934, Mickey Mouse had become the front-runner in the world of character watches; but many little girls in the 1930s felt they just had to have an Annie wristwatch. The rectangular shape of the Annie watch was also used by New Haven Watch Company for their Dick Tracy and Smitty wristwatches, and the company also produced a Popeye wristwatch and pocket watch.

Orphan Annie and Dick Tracy watch ad from the 1935 Sears Roebuck catalog.

Among the most striking character watches competing with Mickey Mouse in the 1930s were Buck Rogers (Ingraham, 1935), Flash Gordon (Ingersoll, 1939), and Superman (New Haven, 1939). The very first use of a comic character on a timepiece was the Buster Brown pocket watch which was sold at the St. Louis World's Fair in 1904. Ingersoll mass-produced a Buster Brown watch in 1908 and other companies followed suit in 1929 and again, decades later, in the 1970s.

THE STORY OF THE INGERSOLL BROTHERS

In 1880 two brothers from Michigan started the Ingersoll Watch Company in New York City. Robert (age 21) and Charles Ingersoll (age 15) created a pocket watch design and took it to the Waterbury Clock Company, which agreed to produce 12,000 pieces using their design to be sold in the marketplace for $1.50. Three years later the two young men created a pocket watch that could sell for $1. The Ingersoll brothers exhibited their products at the 1893 Chicago World's Fair, where they featured the first commemorative pocket watch—the Chicago World's Fair watch. By 1895 Ingersoll's watch sales hit 15 million and by 1899 Robert Ingersoll sold an order of one million of his dollar watches to Symond's London Shops. Advertising campaigns stated:

ABOVE: *Ingersoll stainless steel pocket watch with second hand, c. 1923.*

LEFT: *Matchbook features Ingersoll's Aero wristwatch and Yankee pocket watch with lapel cord.*

"Ingersoll—the watch that made a dollar famous."

Likeness of the Ingersoll brothers as youngsters advertising pocket watches in a 1923 ad.

By the end of World War I, 50 million Ingersoll watches had been sold in the United States and around the globe. Mark Twain, Thomas Edison, and Theodore Roosevelt wore Ingersolls. On one of Roosevelt's forays into Africa, he met a native who sported an Ingersoll watch of his own which he had acquired in a trading of tribal goods with a tourist. The native called the former president "the man who came from the land of Ingersoll." In 1922 the Waterbury Clock Company bought out the Robert H. Ingersoll & Bro. Company, continuing the business under the new name, Ingersoll-Waterbury Company.

In London, Ingersoll Watch Company Limited developed a chain of shops which sold timepieces. The name "Ingersoll" on a watch had proved to be of value in terms of sales and the Waterbury Company continued to utilize this name as a legend on the watches they produced.

Warranty letter from the Ingersoll-Waterbury Company inserted into a 1935 Mickey Mouse wrist-watch box.

THE INGERSOLL-WATERBURY CO.

Ingersoll
Watches and Clocks

WATERBURY
NEW YORK
CHICAGO

SAN FRANCISCO
LONDON
MONTREAL

WATERBURY, CONN.

Dear Customer:

    Should your watch require repair, you will receive more prompt and efficient service by sending it direct to The Ingersoll-Waterbury Co., Waterbury, Conn., as directed by our guarantee. We will return it promptly and we ask that you allow sufficient time for transportation both ways before writing about the date of its return. Please bear in mind that delays may occur in transit for which we are not responsible.

    Your watch should NOT be returned through the dealer from whom it was purchased as this will involve additional handling, resulting in the loss of time. Moreover, if the watch is a wrist model, the strap will have been adjusted to your wrist and cannot be used by anyone else.

    Inside this letter you will find your guarantee which we suggest you read over and preserve. You will also find directions for regulating the watch to your particular conditions and for adjusting bands on wrist watches.

    The Ingersoll name is your assurance that your watch was manufactured with the highest grade materials by expert American workmen following designs laid out by experienced engineers. We are sure that you will be entirely satisfied with your purchase.

3

Very cordially yours,
THE INGERSOLL-WATERBURY CO.
Service Department

1933—THE INGERSOLL MICKEY MOUSE WATCH

First Mickey Mouse wristwatch.

Probably no single product has had more impact in terms of ongoing sales than the first watch to feature Mickey Mouse on its dial. The idea for a Mickey Mouse watch was first developed by Kay Kamen, who sold the concept to the Ingersoll-Waterbury Clock Company. The company later announced that they had been on the brink of bankruptcy, and that Mickey Mouse had saved the day in 1933. *Toys and Novelties* magazine reported under the headline "Glad-handing Mouse Rescues Any and All" that "Toy makers and merchants can point to many instances where, single-handed, Mickey Mouse drove off lurking receivers with the same vigor he exerts in defending Minnie in the movies."

An exclusive worldwide contract in perpetuity was given to Ingersoll by Walt Disney Enterprises. Ingersoll also developed an agreement with Sears Roebuck which put forth monies for development, initial expenses, advertising and inventory procedures. The Mickey Mouse wristwatch which initially sold for $3.75 and a pocket watch which sold for $1.50 were packaged in well-designed orange, black and white cardboard boxes featuring Mickey and his early barnyard pals Minnie Mouse, Horace Horsecollar, Pluto the Pup and Clarabelle Cow.

1933 Mickey Mouse wristwatch box.

First Mickey Mouse wristwatch atop original box.

The first animated Ingersoll watches with a white-faced pie-wedge ovular-eyed Mickey pointing at the hours and minutes with his yellow-gloved hands were circular and also featured a tiny rotating second hand with three miniaturized Mickeys who appear to be chasing after one another.

The watch was designed by August Shallack, who worked in advertising for United Artists. The watch design was copyrighted by Walt Disney Enterprises in June 1933.

The original patent for the first Mickey Mouse watch reads:

> A time instrument comprising: a dial having time indicia thereon, rotatable seconds, minute and hour members; a figure mounted on said rotatable seconds and fixed thereto so as to rotate therewith and simulating the body of an animate being; and a time indicator mounted on and rotatable with each said rotatable minute and hour members and simulating a part of said animate being.

Eleven thousand Mickey Mouse wristwatches designed by Shallack were sold on one happy day shortly after they were introduced at Macy's Department Store in New York City. The store featured full window displays of Mickey Mouse wristwatches, pocket watches, electric clocks, and "wagging head" wind-up clocks. At Marshall Field's Department Store in Chicago, Mickey Mouse Ingersoll watches were sold at a spectacular canopied display on the main floor featuring a gigantic Mickey Mouse pocket watch six feet in diameter held up by four three-foot-high Mickey Mouse cut-outs, the whole revolving atop special glass watch counters.

Mickey Mouse watch counter display at Marshall Field's Department Store in Chicago, February 26, 1935.

The Mickey Mouse wristwatches were featured at Ingersoll's display at the Century of Progress Exposition in Chicago in 1933. At this pivotal World's Fair, which introduced Americans to the concept of modernism, Ingersoll established a mini-factory where visitors to the fair could order a watch, see it created and receive it right away. The Mickey Mouse watch outsold a special World's Fair commemorative watch by a three-to-one margin. The Mickey watch, which had initially been thought to be just a novelty, became *the* thing to wear at the Fair, in Chicago, and, ultimately, across America.

ABOVE: *The swirling comet which adorns this enameled license plate souvenir was the official symbol of the 1933–34 Chicago Exposition, the first "modern" World's Fair.*

RIGHT: *Drawing that accompanied original patent application for a Mickey Mouse time instrument, filed May 22, 1933.*

BELOW: *Article from* Your Plant *magazine.*

After just eight weeks of production the Mickey Mouse *number one* watch proved such a success that a contemporary trade magazine, *Your Plant*, reported in April 1935 that Ingersoll added 2,800 new employees to its 200-person work force, a very rare occurrence during the Great Depression. Two and one-half million of these watches were sold between June 1933 and June 1935 and the company happily paid Disney a quarter of a million dollars in

licensing fees. By 1939 Mickey Mouse pointing out the time on a watch had become such an integral part of American culture that a Mickey watch was put in a permanently sealed time capsule at the 1939 New York World's Fair. The Mickey Mouse watch had become an American icon.

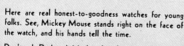

Mickey Mouse Magazine inside cover ad featuring watch styles available in December 1938.

The August 1933 issue of *Playthings* magazine, in a feature, "Mickey Mouse Tells Time," declared Mickey timepieces the "official timekeeper for boys and girls." Kids began asking for Mickey watches for Christmas and upon graduation. Parents obliged, and some took to wearing these big-sized watches themselves. In Hollywood a Mickey Mouse watch became a glamorous accessory for movie stars including Shirley Temple, Jane Withers, Mary Pickford, Dick Powell, and Janet Gaynor. The famous Dionne Quintuplets, all identical girls, were given free Mickey Mouse watches by Ingersoll. It was reported that even the mysterious Greta Garbo owned one.

Colorful, forthright and charming Ingersoll advertisements for Mickey watches were common through the 1930s. Ads targeted for children began appearing in strategic publications like *Mickey Mouse Magazine*, *Famous Funnies*, *Comic Weekly*, the *Dell Super Comic Group*, and in Sunday newspaper comic supplements.

A 1937 Ingersoll ad featured a Mickey Mouse DeLuxe wristwatch with a chain-link band and Minnie Mouse and Donald Duck "charm" bracelets for just $3.95. The leather band Mickey Mouse wristwatch was offered at $3.25. The Mickey Mouse lapel watch, regarded by watch collectors as the most beautiful of the Mickey Mouse timepieces, could be bought for $1.50.

Mickey Mouse Magazine *ad for Ingersoll wristwatch.*

LEFT: *Mickey Mouse wristwatch illustration with limerick from* Your Plant *magazine, April 1935.*

Hickory dickory dock
Mickey's on the clock!
His cheerful grin
Brings orders in
Hickory dickory dock!

Walt Disney became the official chairman of a committee created by Kay Kamen to launch a national Mickey Mouse Watch Window Contest. This trim-a-store-window contest centered around the Mickey Mouse watch ran from July 15 to November 15, 1937. Entrants were advised in a two-page ad in July of 1937 that after creating these special windows they could send in snapshots of the displays. Contestants were informed that they could use other Mickey Mouse toys and dolls to highlight the watches. The awards were to be judged by a jury of eight notables consisting of:

Litho-on-cardboard die-cut counter display with Mickey holding an original Mickey Mouse watch.

Walt Disney,
        Creator of Mickey Mouse, *Hollywood*

Kay Kamen,
        President of Walt Disney Enterprises, *New York*

Chas. J. Heale,
        Editor of Hardware Age, *New York*

A. Merchant Clark,
        Editor of The Jeweler's Circular, *Keystone, New York*

Louis J. F. Moore,
        Editor of American Druggist, *New York*

J.M. Shearman,
        President, Hardware World, *Chicago*

Jerry McQuade,
        Editor of Drug Topics, *New York*

Harry J. Bromley,
        Vice President, National Jeweler

The windows proved to be a great sales gimmick. Mickey Mouse watches fostered business in jewelry, drug and general stores across America. Mickey Mouse became a hero in the thirties, lauded by *The New York Times* for rescuing the Lionel Corporation (the Lionel Mickey Mouse handcar was a huge success) and the Ingersoll-Waterbury Clock Company.

The original Mickey Mouse watches were durable and were made with a reliable pin lever movement developed during World War I for the U.S. Army and Navy. One legend has it that the Ingersoll-Waterbury Clock Company had crates full of surplus military watches in storage and simply added the Mickey Mouse image to the watch face. This account, however, has never been confirmed. Accurate facts about the history of early Mickey Mouse watches are difficult to find. A flood in the 1950s in Waterbury, Connecticut, destroyed factory records.

"Win $250"—Mickey Mouse Watch Window Trim Contest ad, 1937.

Mickey Mouse watches advertised in the 1935 Kay Kamen Mickey Mouse Merchandise catalog.

The Ten Most Collectible Mickey Mouse Watches from the 1930s

1 9 3 3—The Ingersoll-Waterbury Clock Company began production of the first Mickey Mouse watches in June 1933. By December of that year 900,000 had been sold. The first Mickey watches are considered to be ones produced during the first year. In a chromium plated case, the watch has a 1 $^{1}/_{16}$" round face diameter with a circular dial. Labeled on the righthand side of the watch is:

MICKEY
MOUSE
INGERSOLL
©

The paper face of the watch has a full-figured image of Mickey Mouse with bowlegs (to allow for the second hand), wearing red shorts, yellow gloves and shoes. The hands of the watch serve as Mickey's arms and he is looking at the number 1 on the dial. The second hand is a tiny circular revolving disk featuring three tiny Mickeys chasing each other. They all have red shorts, yellow gloves and shoes. A unique animated effect is achieved with the racing second hand in conjunction with the ticking movement of Mickey's hands and arms.

First Mickey Mouse wristwatch with chrome-link band.

*1933 Mickey Mouse
wristwatch in box.*

The wristwatch came with a chromium plated metal link band, the first link on either side of the watch case featuring an embossed image of Mickey. The watch also came with a black leather band featuring the same "Mickey link" appliqués on the band at each side of the watch face. Some of these embossed "charms" were highlighted with a touch of black paint. The wristwatches were originally packaged in a rectangular box with black and white cartoon images of Mickey, Minnie, Pluto, Horace and Clarabelle featured in the design. A rare version of the orange box features just a large image of Mickey in a circle on the box top. The original cost was $3.75.

*Underside of Mickey
Mouse Ingersoll
wristwatch box.*

1934—In 1934, Ingersoll-Waterbury manufactured the exact same watch, but added the words:

MADE
IN
USA

Located next to the number 8 on the dial, the imprint was deemed necessary to discourage counterfeits and to increase foreign sales. Other changes in 1934 included a lower price of $2.98 through Sears Roebuck & Co. mail-order catalogs. The original orange box was replaced with a larger cardboard box with a single red, yellow, black and white image of Mickey Mouse standing on a red banner which proclaimed: "Ingersoll Mickey Mouse Wristwatch." Inside is a similar Mickey image wherein two open slots are utilized to contain and display the watch as if Mickey were holding it up between his two hands.

1933—First produced by Ingersoll-Waterbury in 1933, the Mickey Mouse pocket watch came with a chromium watch fob imprinted with an image of Mickey, attached with a leather strap. The image of Mickey Mouse on the face of the pocket watch is the same as the design on the wristwatch. It also had the revolving second hand disc with three tiny Mickeys chasing after each other. A die-embossed Mickey Mouse image is imprinted on

Mickey Mouse wristwatch with chrome-link band and die-cut metal Mickey Mouse appliqués.

the back of the pocket watch which also carries the names "Mickey Mouse" and "Ingersoll." Two types of pocket watches were offered, one with a long stem and one with a short stem. They were packaged in the same kind of box as the Number One.

1935—The Ingersoll-Waterbury Mickey Mouse lapel watch, first offered in 1935, has a bright Mickey Mouse figure against a white background in his usual outfit of red shorts, yellow gloves and shoes, identical to the wrist and pocket watches.

Mickey Mouse pocket watch with leather strap and round metal fob.

The lapel watch is, in fact, a pocket watch but without the second hand. The case is gleaming black enamel with a thick silk cord meant to be affixed to a lapel. The watch can then be dropped into the breast pocket of a man's or lady's suit. Women who bought these beautiful watches often carried them in their purses. Many collectors consider the lapel watch to be the most attractive of the 1930s Mickey Mouse timepieces. By 1938 the image of Mickey on the lapel watch was redesigned with a shorter snout and smaller balloon ears.

Ad from Mickey Mouse Magazine *for the lapel watch, March 1938.*

1938—Always looking for something new, consumers soon tired of the original round watch. Ingersoll-Waterbury responded with its 1938 DeLuxe Mickey Mouse wristwatch, manufactured from April 1937 to the fall of 1942. Rectangular, with a chromium case, it featured a straighter-legged, taller figure of Mickey with oval eyes, red pants, yellow shoes, buttons and gloves. The circular second hand disc featured a single rotating Mickey on the run. The watch face is labeled at the top:

MADE IN USA

Below, under Mickey's snout, is:

MICKEY
MOUSE
INGERSOLL
©
W. D. ENT.

DeLuxe Mickey Mouse wrist-watch with plain link band, 1938.

The attractive packaging has a box cover featuring Mickey in a high hat, leaning on a walking stick (and wearing his own wristwatch). The pie-wedge indentation on his eyes has been altered to two black ovals. On the box Mickey is wearing orange shoes (though with yellow gloves) and is standing on a platform with a scroll scripted: "Ingersoll." The display on the inside repeats the high-hat Mickey image, with Mickey this time holding the actual watch in his hands. The inside display reads "$3.95" in one area and under the Mickey image: "Ingersoll" and "Mickey Mouse—DeLuxe Wrist Watch." It came with a leather band and later with a plain link band adorned with chromium "charms" of Minnie and Donald on the links closest to the watchface.

A real watch is attached to this 1938 die-cut cardboard store display sign which heralds the "New Ingersoll Mickey Mouse DeLuxe Wrist Watch."

"High-Hat" Mickey DeLuxe wristwatch in box.

*The Mickey Mouse wristwatch for 1939 has a plain
second hand and leather wristband.*

1939—Making use of the same image of Mickey as the 1938
model, the Mickey Mouse wristwatch for 1939 added new fluting
on the sides of the chromium case, and the second-hand disc
with Mickey was replaced with one bearing
the numbers 15, 30, 45, and 60. Larger,
more legible numbers were used on the dial
and the watch was offered with a plain
black leather band.

*Ingersoll watch ad
features DeLuxe wrist-
watch with charms and
lapel watch, late 1930s.*

1939—For the first time, in
1939, and for just $1 more, Ingersoll
offered a limited edition 14-carat rolled
gold plate "Gold Tone" model Mickey
Mouse wristwatch. This watch was
offered with a plain brown leather
wristband. The gold tone watch was
later offered at the same price as
the chromium watch.

1934—The first English Mickey Mouse pocket watch came with a die-embossed back and was marketed by Ingersoll Ltd. of London. It featured a full Mickey image with thin, straight legs, wearing bulbous shorts and small shoes. The hands, in orange gloves, are five-fingered. The second hand features three tiny walking Mickeys. There are designations on the watch face for military time (i.e., a small 13 appears above the number 1, a small 14 appears above the number 2, and so forth). The words inscribed on the watch face read:

MICKEY
MOUSE
INGERSOLL

At the bottom, under the figure of Mickey, is the word:

FOREIGN

First English Mickey Mouse pocket watch with leather strap and fancy enameled fob.

Mickey Mouse English pocket watch, second issue.
Note five-fingered hand and "five o'clock shadow," 1934.

1 9 3 6—Ingersoll Ltd. of London issued a second English Mickey Mouse pocket watch without the die-embossed back.

1 9 3 4—The same image of Mickey on the first English pocket watch was reduced by Ingersoll, Ltd. for their Mickey Mouse wristwatch, which also included the military time designations. Though the English Mickey Mouse wristwatch is somewhat smaller than the American version, larger ones turn up as well, adding to the confusion of which came first. Some collectors regard the English watch as better than the American counterpart in terms of design, but this is always a matter of personal choice and preference. In England in the Depression, pocket watches in general were popular but wristwatches continued to grow in sales in the mid to late 1930s. All the English wristwatch bands were plain leather straps without any Mickey charms on them.

Mickey Mouse English wristwatch, 1934.

The Lucky Seven—1930s Mickey Mouse Clocks

The first Mickey Mouse electric clock, 1933.

1933—Spray-painted "Depression Green," the first Mickey Mouse electric clock from Ingersoll-Waterbury is 4 1/2 " square. A colorful, decorative paper band (sometimes missing or left off in the manufacturing process) is glued to the outside of the metal clock case featuring Mickey and Minnie Mouse, Pluto the Pup, Horace Horsecollar and Clarabelle Cow. Imprinted on the face of the clock is:

MICKEY
MOUSE
INGERSOLL
©

The patent notice numbers and "Made in U.S.A." appear at the bottom of the clock face. An animated, somersaulting-around-the-dial Mickey has yellow shoes and red or yellow gloves pointing out the time. The square box for the clock has the same pattern design used on the original wristwatch box— the early characters in black and white running around against

41

an orange background. When the box is opened a pop-up die-cut cardboard Mickey holds a placard that reads:

INGERSOLL MICKEY MOUSE CLOCK

The price was $1.50.

1933—The first Mickey Mouse wind-up clock, also produced in 1933 by Ingersoll-Waterbury, is similar in size and color to the electric one with the band around the outside, but features a stationary image of Mickey with his yellow gloved hands pointing to the numerals. The same second hand on the Mickey Mouse wristwatch is enlarged to scale for the Mickey Mouse wind-up clock.

1934—Adding to the company's clock roster, Ingersoll produced the first Mickey Mouse "wagging head" alarm clock when they realized they had forgotten to include an alarm in their 1933 models. In addition to a 30-hour wind-up movement, the clock featured a special movement that animated Mickey's head. Mickey points out the time with red-gloved hands. The round clock came in "Depression Green" or bright red and sold for $1.50. The Sears Roebuck catalog offered it for $1.39.

The "wagging head" wind-up alarm clock.

*Rare Art Deco wind-up desk clock only two inches high featuring
Bakelite case and celluloid crystal. From Ingersoll, 1934.*

1933—Produced by Ingersoll, Ltd. of London, the English
wind-up clock included a second hand feature with three, or in
some cases, two Mickeys.

1933—Ingersoll Ltd. of London's English alarm clock is similar
in style to the English wind-up, only it has an alarm.
Note: Ingersoll Ltd. of London also imported and sold
American-made Ingersolls including the Mickey Mouse watches
and the electric clock. The English clocks are labeled
"Made in the U.S.A." on the face of the dial, even though
they were manufactured in Great Britain.

1934—Rarest of all Mickey Mouse clocks is a two-inch-high
wind-up Art-Deco style desk clock with a square celluloid clock
face in a green Bakelite case. The circular second hand is a three-
Mickey movement. Made by Ingersoll-Waterbury.

1936—The Bayard Company of France produced a beautiful "wagging head" Mickey Mouse wind-up alarm clock. The Mickey figure on the clock appears to be running and he wears red gloves, yellow shoes and red shorts with yellow buttons. The round metal case was available originally in gray, green, white or red. The words:

BAYARD MICKEY

are imprinted on the face of the dial. "Par authorization Walt Disney—Made in France" appears on the face of the clocks manufactured after World War II. This clock is thought to have been in production from 1936 up through 1969, although the company was officially licensed only in 1947.

Mickey Mouse "wagging head" wind-up clock,
Bayard Company, made in France.

WHO'S AFRAID OF THE BIG BAD WOLF?

No one will ever know to what extent Disney's Three Little Pigs *may be held responsible for pulling America out of the Depression, but certainly the lyrical jeer at the Big Bad Wolf contributed not a little to the raising of people's spirits and to their defiance of circumstance.*

–R. D. Feild,
The Art of Walt Disney
(Macmillan, 1942)

The Silly Symphony color cartoon—*Three Little Pigs*—opened on May 27, 1933 at Radio City Music Hall. *Three Little Pigs* received an Academy Award® for the Disney Studio as Best Cartoon Short Subject of 1932-1933. The song *Who's Afraid of the Big Bad Wolf?* written by Frank Churchill became a hit during the Depression and was recorded by orchestras like Ben Bernie's and played by dance bands at fashionable hotels in America and England. The designs for the Three Little Pigs and Big Bad Wolf wristwatch and pocket watch were patented on February 5, 1934 and a patent for the design for the Three Little Pigs–Big Bad

Wolf alarm clock was granted on July 17, 1934. Watch collectors and dealers today regard these 1930s pieces as among the most stunning and interesting Disney timepieces ever produced. With their bright scarlet background, the graphics are superb examples of cartoon art used on a product. The pocket watch is unusual in that the wolf's eyes blink. It also

RIGHT:
Big Bad Wolf pocket watch fob.

BELOW:
Big Bad Wolf alarm clock with animated jaws.

features the three pigs— Practical Pig, Fifer Pig and Fiddler Pig—and the back is embossed with an image of the Big Bad Wolf. It came with an enameled metal fob attached with a strap of leather that depicted the Three Little Pigs and the words "Who's Afraid of the Big Bad Wolf."

The Big Bad Wolf alarm clock has a full-bodied, furry image of the wolf in the center of

the clock face. He appears to be chasing after his prey with animated jaws that open and close. The alarm clock has "Who's Afraid of the Big Bad Wolf" imprinted on it. The wristwatch has a plain circular second hand; and an attractive chromium link band with an embossed metal

"charm" of the head and jaws of the wolf on one side of the watch face and the Three Little Pigs on the other. All of these were introduced by Ingersoll in 1934. The wristwatch was advertised in the 1935 Sears Roebuck catalog for $2.98 with either a chromium link or leather band; the pocket watch and one of two different fobs for $1.39; and the alarm clock for $1.39. The Big Bad Wolf timepieces are highly sought-after Disney items in today's watch/collectibles marketplace.

ABOVE: *1935 Sears Roebuck catalog ad for Big Bad Wolf timepieces.*

LEFT: *Big Bad Wolf Ingersoll wristwatch, 1934.*

DONALD DUCK MARKS TIME

Donald Duck made his first appearance in the Silly Symphony cartoon *The Wise Little Hen*, released on June 9, 1934. He became Mickey Mouse's popular sidekick and foil in *Orphan's Benefit* and *The Dognapper* in 1934, *On Ice* and *The Band Concert* in 1935, *Mickey's Circus* in 1936 and *Clock Cleaners* in 1937.

In 1935 a Donald Duck wristwatch was manufactured but was never mass produced or distributed. One theory has it that these watches may have been held back in the 1930s with the fear that Donald Duck might cut into the phenomenon of the Mickey Mouse watch marketplace. Ingersoll's first Donald Duck

Donald Duck wristwatch manufactured by Ingersoll features Mickey Mouse chrome-link band and Mickey Mouse second hand. This example is missing one wing.

wristwatch features a figure of Donald holding red flags pointing to the numerals. On the original prototypes the revolving circular disc second hand features three tiny racing Donald Ducks; later this rare second hand was replaced by the more familiar one with three racing Mickeys. The original had enameled metal "charms" of Donald on the wristband, that were also replaced by the Mickeys featured on the original Mickey Mouse wristwatch.

The Donald Duck wristwatch, with Donald or Mickey accessories, is extremely rare and collector Hy Brown in his book *Comic Character Timepieces* describes the instance of a Chicago collector purchasing a Donald Duck wristwatch prototype, mint-in-the-original-box at the Brimfield, Massachusetts, flea market for a record $6,000.

Donald Duck pocket watch box, 1939.

The Donald Duck pocket watch, produced by Ingersoll in 1939, fared better in the marketplace, but was not as popular as a Mickey Mouse or Big Bad Wolf pocket watch. On the pocket watch Donald's hands are on his hips and the clock's hands are traditional arrows. The second hand on the pocket watch is plain; "© 1939 W. D. Prod." is imprinted on the torso of the Duck and at the bottom of the watch face is "Made in U.S.A." The pocket watch does not say "Ingersoll" but the wristwatch is labeled: "Donald Duck Ingersoll ©." Some models of the Donald pocket watch have a Mickey Mouse image on the reverse side. However, in today's collectibles market the 1930s Donald Duck wristwatch and the Donald Duck pocket watch are prized precisely because of their limited sales and limited production.

ABOVE: Donald Duck Ingersoll pocket watch.

RIGHT: Donald Duck checks out the time on a lapel watch. Illustration from 1938 Mickey Mouse Magazine.

Clock Cleaners

Mickey Mouse and Donald Duck in the 1937 Disney cartoon Clock Cleaners, Good Housekeeping, *June 1937.*

The 1937 Disney cartoon short **Clock Cleaners** is a fun-slam-bang-tick-tock ***tour de farce*** that has Mickey Mouse and Donald Duck as amateur clock cleaners up against an almost Rube Goldberg time machine that has gone haywire and cuckoo crazy. Donald and Mickey, like Laurel and Hardy, are perfect foils for one another in a hilarious one-of-a-kind romp where they are playing with the concept of time itself—represented here as a beat-up old grandfather clock.

1940s

MICKEY MOUSE
TIME – W.W. II AND
THE POSTWAR ERA

New production of all Disney watches ceased during the World War II years 1941 to 1945. Ingersoll-Waterbury Clock Company continued in business until 1944. Its factories were taken over by U.S. Time, which had opened its headquarters plant in nearby Middlebury, Connecticut in 1942; and by 1951 Ingersoll-Waterbury was completely absorbed by U.S. Time.

United States Time Corporation, with sales headquarters in Rockefeller Center at 630 Fifth Avenue, continued to use the known Ingersoll name on their Disney character watches. To preview their first postwar Disney watches, U.S. Time took out a double-page advertisement in the July 1945 issue of *American Druggist* magazine (periodical for pharmacists still published). Under the slogan "The World's Largest Manufacturer of Watches and Clocks" the ad was headlined:

OPPOSITE:
1947–48 Walt Disney Character Merchandise catalog from Kay Kamen Ltd., New York.

Mickey is surrounded by his friends in this U.S. Time ad that appeared in American Druggist, July 1945.

WOW! WHAT A SALES FORCE! Mickey Mouse and HIS WHOLE GANG will soon help you sell U.S. Time Products.

BEFORE THE WAR, Ingersoll Mickey Mouse wrist watches, pocket watches and clocks had become an American tradition.

Pretty soon now, not only Mickey but his whole gang . . .

Donald Duck, Pluto, Minnie Mouse, Joe Carioca, Snow White and the Seven Dwarfs, all of Disney's delightful crew . . . will appear on vastly improved Ingersolls . . . much handsomer, tougher, more accurate.

These new timepieces will reflect the great war-born achievement of U.S. Time, the makers of Ingersoll. That achievement is the mass production of precision parts. It will enable you to offer your customers a complete line of beautiful, high-precision timepieces at popular prices.

The illustration depicts Mickey Mouse, Minnie Mouse, Panchito, José Carioca, Dopey, Pluto, Snow White and all Seven Dwarfs showing the forthcoming watches.

In the fall of 1946 U.S. Time introduced a small square-dial Mickey Mouse wristwatch under the brand name of Kelton, which featured just the head of Mickey rotating on a post as the hour hand turned. It was produced for one year with the Kelton brand name on the watch face and "U.S. Time" on the back.

ABOVE: *Page from jeweler's catalog offering the post-war Mickey Mouse and Donald Duck wristwatches.*

LEFT: *The Kelton Mickey Mouse wristwatch, 1946.*

THE FIRST POSTWAR INGERSOLL WATCH

In December of 1946 (through the winter of 1949) U.S. Time offered its first postwar Ingersoll Mickey Mouse wristwatch. Rectangular, and without a second hand, it was imprinted on the front: "Ingersoll © WDP" and on the back "U.S. Time." The figure of Mickey Mouse was redesigned and shows Mickey with pupils in his eyes. The original cost was $6.95.

U.S. Time introduced a round dial version of the watch in 1947 with a white background and red

Ingersoll

MICKEY MOUSE WRIST WATCH

US TIME

numbers. It was imprinted "Ingersoll © WDP" on the watch face and "U.S. Time" on the back. They then offered one with a 3/4" diameter from 1950 through 1960. There were two Donald Duck wristwatches on the market in 1947, 1" round in diameter with a blue face and chromium case and the "New Donald Duck Wrist Watch" which was rectangular and also had a blue face ($1 more for a gold-tone case). A companion watch featuring Daisy Duck was also offered in 1947 for the same $6.95 price.

Mickey Mouse's 20th Birthday

In 1947 in anticipation of the premiere of *So Dear to My Heart* and Mickey Mouse's 20th birthday, U.S. Time advertised two special series of Disney character watches. Consisting of four watches in rectangular chromium cases (similar to the 1947 Mickey, Donald and Daisy cases), the first group highlights Danny, the central character in *So Dear to My Heart*.

OPPOSITE: *"New Donald Duck Wrist Watch" 1947 box insert display card.*

LEFT: *Donald Duck wristwatch, 1947.*

BELOW: *Bobby Driscoll and Luana Patten, who appeared together in the films* Song of the South *and* So Dear to My Heart, *here shown in advertisement wearing Mickey Mouse wristwatches.*

Mother...

will they be **PUNCTUAL** citizens?

MICKEY MOUSE WATCH

DANNY

GIFT PACKED

$4.95
SUGGESTED RETAIL PRICE

LOUIE

BRIGHT CHROME CASE

TOP: *1947 Ingersoll Special Series of four character watches featured Snow White, Louie, Little Pig and Danny.*

ABOVE: *Danny Ingersoll wristwatch.*

RIGHT: *Louie wristwatch.*

This nostalgic film about farm life in Missouri was one of Walt Disney's favorites. Danny the mischievous black lamb kicks up on a bright orange watch face; the companion watches feature Snow White, Louie, and Little Pig. The suggested retail price for these watches, which came with a junior-size leather wristband, was $4.95 each.

Introducing the ten watches in the new Birthday Series, U.S. Time hailed them as the "Technicolor Hit of the Season!" The 1948 series,

all in round chromium cases and several featuring "luminescent" paint on the watch hands, had Mickey Mouse leading off a parade which included Pluto and Bambi (with luminescent ears), Jiminy Cricket, Pinocchio, Dopey, José Carioca (also known as Joe Carioca), Donald Duck, Daisy Duck and Bongo—The Wonder Bear, a new character introduced in the live action/animated picture *Fun and Fancy Free.*

TOP: *Little Pig wristwatch.*

LEFT: *Snow White wristwatch.*

animate your

Mickey Mouse

Daisy Duck

Pluto

Joe Carioca

Bambi

this is an *Ingersoll* presentation!

retail price $6.95 *plus 10% fed.tax*

In 1947 there were 14,438,709 birthdays for youngsters* from 5 to 10 years old.

5–6 years	5,322,423
7–8 years	4,625,987
8–10 years	4,490,299

(*already sold on these lovable Walt Disney characters!)

"Animate Your Cash Register in '48!"— ad featuring all ten of the Birthday Series watches.

All ten watches were featured in a large, colorful counter display box with all the characters centered around an ebullient Mickey Mouse, who is depicted holding his own birthday cake. Department stores created special sections with displays of Mickey and a full array of the new character watches. A special sign at the May Company watch counter in Los Angeles proclaimed:

"Ingersoll and Walt Disney get together again. It's their first showing in the United States of New Watches—$6.95 (plus 10% Federal tax) at May Co. Wilshire"

cash register in '48!

With Ten Famous Walt Disney characters on the most famous children's watches in the world! In Technicolor!

Bongo

Pinocchio

Jiminy Cricket

Donald Duck

Dopey

The Walt Disney birthday gift promotion
Increases the big market created by Mickey Mouse.
Is a twelve-month "candle power" plan for sales.
Is gay, colourful, educational — makes telling time fun
Moves fast—you know kids: if one gets a Walt Disney
watch, every kid in town has to have one — or else!
Cashes in with a full selection of models. (Nationally
advertised, increases turnover, reduces sales costs)

offer #400 ...

The characters on the watch faces of the 1949 "luminous dial with luminous hands" models are larger than the images on the 1948 models. The images step out of the inner circle and some characters are not represented in the new lineup. Intrepid watch collector Hy Brown cites that although all ten characters are seen in 1949 advertisements, he and other avid Disney watch collectors have only found seven in the collector field. The Birthday Series watches came in identical red lithographed cardboard boxes featuring all the characters with Mickey Mouse. A special

OVERLEAF: 1948 Birthday Series, wristwatches, are clockwise from the top left: Mickey, Pluto, Daisy, Bambi, Pinocchio, Donald, Bongo, and José Carioca.

63

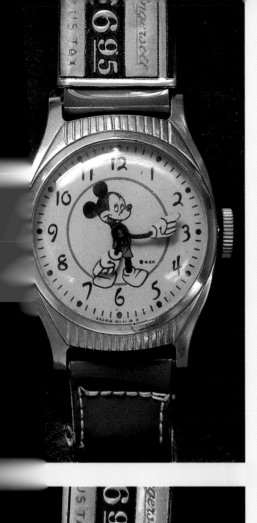

plastic "Birthday Box" in the shape of a
cake "with real candles that light" and a
"sterling silver" ring *and* a brightly colored
ballpoint pen with decals of Mickey or Donald
were offered with the watches for just $7.95.

The sterling silver adjustable rings with
four different Walt Disney characters including
Mickey and Donald were on a luminous back-

ground that glowed in the dark and sold separately for $1.50. The clip-on petite ballpoints sold for $1. These pens and rings were also offered as premiums when you bought the new Celcon ivory Mickey Mouse clock put out by U.S. Time in 1949. This attractive clock features a 40-hour movement with one key that winds both the clock and alarm. It came in a colorful gift box and sold for $3.45.

Ingersoll/U.S. Time Mickey Mouse alarm clock for 1949 had a Celcon ivory case, 40-hour all-metal movement, a melodious bell and a muffled tick, all for $3.45.

MICKEY MOUSE ALARM CLOCK *Ingersoll*

attractive gift box

Colorful Mickey Mouse tells time with his hands on this Celcon ivory clock. 40 hour all-metal movement— one key winds both clock and alarm— melodious bell—muffled tick

$3.45 plus fed. tax
your cost ■■ **$1.97**

US TIME CORPORATION **PRIZE AND PREMIUM DIVISION**
The United States Time Corporation
630 Fifth Avenue · New York 20, N. Y.

Walt Disney *Character*
MERCHANDISE
1949 – 1950

Copyright Walt Disney Productions

KAY KAMEN LTD
1270 AVENUE OF THE AMERICAS, NEW YORK, 20, N. Y., U.S.A.
LICENSING REPRESENTATIVES FOR THE COPYRIGHTED
WALT DISNEY CHARACTERS

yright W

1950s

T.V. AND THE THEME PARK ERA

OPPOSITE:
1949–50 Walt Disney Character Merchandise catalog from Kay Kamen, Ltd., New York.

LEFT: *1950s Mickey Mouse watch disc.*

BELOW:
The 1950s Mickey Mouse Ingersoll wristwatch, produced by U.S. Time.

By the 1950s Mickey Mouse—the teller of time—had become a celebrated and timeless character. Mickey—in person—functioned as the official host and goodwill ambassador when Disneyland—the first theme park—opened on July 17, 1955 in California. The Mickey Mouse Club, which premiered on October 3, 1955 on the ABC Network, became a phenomenal success with the Mouseketeers ending each show singing the jingle—"M-I-C-K-E-Y M-O-U-S-E!"

U.S. Time produced the most popular of the Mickey Mouse watches of the 1950s (from 1957 through 1960). The legend "U.S. Time" was embossed on the back of the watch case. This Ingersoll had a dial one inch in diameter, a white background

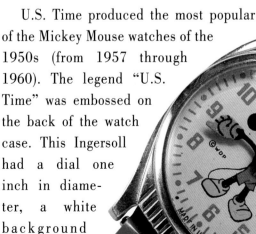

with red numbers; but had no second hand. A full image of Mickey Mouse points to the hour and the minute. On the watch face are the identifications: "Ingersoll," "© WDP" and "Made in U.S. A." The 1950 watch came in a flat box that was similar to the packaging used for the 1947 model. The price in the early 50s was $6.95; but it was later sold for $7.95. Starting in 1958 they offered a plastic or porcelain figurine of Mickey or Minnie with the watch as part of the packaging.

A similar model was produced from 1950 to 1960 that was slightly smaller in size ($3/4$" in diameter). A *Life* magazine double-page ad (December 8, 1952) promoted the '52 reissue of this watch for Christmas. The Disney character "sterling" rings and ballpoint pens were advertised in the same ad. These were often given away as watch premiums and sometimes sold for $1.50 for the ring and $1 for the pen with the purchase of a Mickey Mouse watch. The attractive Ingersoll ivory Celcon plastic Mickey Mouse alarm clock was also

"New Mickey Mouse Wrist Watch"—flattened cardboard box.

WALT DISNEY'S
Mickey Mouse

$7 95
30071

available in 1952 for $3.45. The striking full-color *Life* magazine advertisement which depicts an actual size watch is a collectible itself in the paper ephemera and Disneyana marketplace. The ad has the Ingersoll logo in red script in prominent large letter format and "U.S. Time Corporation" in a tiny square box in the lower right-hand corner.

In 1955 the Mickey Mouse watch was issued in a red plastic watch case with a red "vinylite" wristband backed-up with "real leather" on the inside. There was also a Donald Duck companion watch that came

with a blue band—both were packaged in identical red or blue hinged plastic pop-up boxes. On Wednesday, March 27, 1957 in Disneyland, U.S. Time officials presented Walt Disney with the 25-millionth Mickey Mouse watch.

ABOVE: *A jovial Mickey Mouse juggles the Ingersoll wristwatches, pens, rings and a clock in a stunning double-page* Life *magazine Christmas advertisement, December 8, 1952.*

OPPOSITE: *Mickey Mouse wristwatch sold for $7.95 and came with a porcelain Mickey figurine in 1958.*

LEFT: *The Ingersoll Mickey Mouse wristwatch, U.S. Time ad.*

The United States Time Corporation
International Building, Rockefeller Center, New York

Alice in Wonderland

Mickey Mouse

Ingersoll®

Character Watche

$5.30

$7.95

SHOCK RESISTANT

CHROME-PLATED BEZELS

STAINLESS STEEL BACKS

UNBREAKABLE MAINSPRINGS

© WALT DISNEY PRODUCTIONS

Beautifully molded Character Watch Figurines of Alice in Wonderland, Cinderella, Mickey Mouse, and Snow White are packaged with each of these character watches. These fine figurines, which are five inches tall, add extra value to these watches and make them exciting gifts for boys and girls.

30011 — Alice in Wonderland—B
30031 — Cinderella—Pink Strap
30071 — Mickey Mouse—Red Str
30081 — Snow White—Yellow St
**The consumer prices are the minimum Fair Trad
those states having Fair Trade laws.

UNITED STATES TIME CORPORATION   Sales Headquarters—375 Park Avenue, New Yo

Calling All Girls:
Cinderella, Alice in Wonderland, Snow White, Daisy Duck & Minnie Mouse Time

While women and girls certainly wore Mickey Mouse wristwatches, Snow White, Cinderella, Alice in Wonderland, Daisy Duck, and Minnie Mouse watches have been worn exclusively by females.

Certainly a Cinderella watch is among the most popular Disney watches of all time. In the 1950s, wearing a Cinderella watch was regarded as a status symbol; and every young lady who wore one identified with the magic of the Cinderella story.

Alice in Wonderland on a watch did not captivate in the same sense that Cinderella did; but in today's watch collectibles marketplace a hard-to-find Alice watch is considered very desirable. Collector-writer Robert Lesser in his book *A Celebration of Comic Art and Memorabilia* regards the watch as a rarity and as a most attractive collector's item.

ABOVE: *The* Blanche Neige *alarm clock from Reveil Bayard was produced in France in 1969.*

OPPOSITE: *Ingersoll Character Watches featuring the names of Alice in Wonderland, Snow White, Cinderella, and Mickey Mouse. Devoid of images, these watches were sold with porcelain or hard plastic figurines.*

The Cinderella wristwatch was originally packaged in an attractive box that portrays scenes from the movie. Inside is the centerpiece—a "glass" slipper (actually clear Lucite plastic) utilized to display the watch. The 1950 Timex watch originally sold for $6.95. Later it was offered with a porcelain or hard plastic figurine of Cinderella.

1950 Cinderella wristwatch.

1950 The new Ingersoll Timex from U.S. Time—full figure—attached to dainty slipper in clear or gold plastic—packaged in round and square boxes featuring scenes from *Cinderella*—originally $6.95—$7.95 later.

1961 "Cinderella" on watch face, no image (part of series)—sold with porcelain or plastic figurine of Cinderella—Timex.

1970 Figure of Cinderella running down the steps of the castle—sold with porcelain or plastic figurine of Cinderella—Timex.

1972 Cinderella bust on a watch face with castle—Bradley.

1984 Quartz LCD—Cinderella and castle with white background on 3/4" watch face—light blue plastic band—$17—Bradley.

1987 Cinderella with pink plastic case and matching plastic band—Lorus.

1990s Cinderella—exclusive to the Disney Store—$19. Cinderella—depicts Cinderella and Prince Charming seated—packaged in a "book," edition of 7,500—Walt Disney Classic Limited Edition Watch Series II—$70.

1950 Cinderella wristwatch in box with cel illustration.

The original Timex Alice in Wonderland wristwatch is somewhat rare. Produced in 1950, it was packaged with a Lucite teacup and later with either a porcelain or molded hard plastic figurine. An unusual 1955 Alice wristwatch is animated with the Mad Hatter on the second hand crazily rocking back and forth. This handsome timepiece was produced by the New Haven Watch Company.

Alice in Wonderland wristwatch with hard plastic figurine sold for $7.95.

1950 Full figure of Alice—packaged in plastic teacup—Timex (U.S. Time).

1955 Alice with animated Mad Hatter rocking back and forth on second hand—New Haven Watch Company.

1960 The words "Alice in Wonderland" on watch face—no image (part of series)— sold with porcelain or hard plastic figurine—Timex.

1970 Alice's head peering through pink flowers— ceramic or plastic figurine—$7.95—Timex.

1972 Reissue of Alice with animated Mad Hatter—Bradley.

1990s Alice's White Rabbit—depicts White Rabbit holding his own pocket watch—limited edition of 7,500—packaged in a "book"—Walt Disney Classic Limited Edition Watch Series II—$70.

Alice in Wonderland wristwatch, Timex, 1970.

Among the most enduring of the feminine Disney princess characters is Snow White, who appeared in the first animated feature-length Disney film, *Snow White and the Seven Dwarfs*, which premiered in Hollywood on December 21, 1937. The raven-haired "fairest of them all" entered the magic kingdom of watches, becoming a perennial popular choice for

Snow White wristwatch, 1950.

many young girls. The most beautiful and collectible of the Snow White wristwatches were issued between 1947 and 1950.

1947 Full figure of Snow White—rectangular—in series of four which included Little Pig, Louie and Danny—U.S. Time—Ingersoll. This earliest Snow White wristwatch has the dainty princess lifting her skirt as if to curtsy. Inside the original box was a reproduction of a movie cel.

1949 Snow White figure based on Gustave Tenggren design—3/4" dial—rectangular or round—$6.95—U.S. Time—Ingersoll.

1950 Snow White on white background— Magic Mirror box—Timex.

1960 Snow White wristwatch had no image but was sold with a porcelain figurine.

1955 Snow White Timex—silver case.

1960 The words "Snow White" only—no image (part of series)—sold with figurine in porcelain or hard plastic—Timex.

1958 Image of Snow White with Dopey—sold with figurine in porcelain or hard plastic—Timex.

1970 Snow White with Dopey—Timex.

1981 Snow White digital—Bradley.

1981 Snow White digital musical alarm—plays "It's A Small World"—Alba.

1987 Snow White 50th Anniversary— white watch face and case—Snow White seated with a blue bird on her right hand with a white ribbed plastic band—Lorus.

1990s Limited Edition—Snow White with revolving Seven Dwarfs.

The "New Donald
Duck Wrist Watch"
boxtop features both
Donald and Daisy
watches.

Donald Duck's girlfriend Daisy Duck first appeared in
the cartoon *Mr. Duck Steps Out* (1940). She was subsequently featured in fourteen films. Originally
Daisy was known as Donna Duck and was first
seen as a señorita in the 1937 cartoon-short
Don Donald. The first Daisy Duck wristwatch
was issued in 1947 and is considered a rare
collector's item today.

1947 Ingersoll Daisy Duck—rectangular—
companion watch to Donald Duck—U.S. Time.

1948 Ingersoll Daisy Duck—round—part
of 20th Birthday Series—U.S. Time.

1949 Ingersoll Daisy Duck—with luminous
hands and luminous outer circle—U.S. Time.

*The first Daisy Duck
wristwatch, 1947.*

Minnie Mouse on a watch did not come into her own until the 1970s nostalgia decade; but Minnie has flourished alongside her companion Mickey ever since. Many young girls and ladies today want their own feminist cartoon character icon and have chosen the independent-minded Minnie to fit the bill.

1971 Timex Minnie Mouse—sold with hard plastic figurine of Mickey Mouse—later models featured a Minnie Mouse figurine—U.S. Time.

1972 Minnie Mouse—Bradley.

1976 Minnie Mouse—Bradley.

1978 Minnie with Mickey—both wearing hats—round watch face—$17.95—Bradley.

1978 Minnie with Mickey playing tennis—$17.95—Bradley.

1978 Minnie with moving head—Bradley.

Minnie Mouse wrist-watch, Timex, 1971.

1978 "Merrie" Mouse—Minnie is wearing a tight skirt with knee-high boots and sports Betty Boop-type spit curls—Bradley.

1980 Disco Minnie and Mickey—with wagging heads and revolving disc—Bradley.

1982 Minnie Mouse—digital—Bradley.

1989 Minnie Mouse necklace watch—Lorus.

1990 Minnie Mouse as "Ginger Rogers"—rectangular gold tone case with expanding metal band—Lorus Quartz.

1991 3-D "talking" Minnie Mouse—companion piece to Mickey Mouse—Sounds Fun, Inc.

Minnie "Ginger Rogers" with floppy hat and fur.

1990s Minnie with Mickey—Snowflake Watch—snowflakes rotate around Minnie and Mickey—1 1/4" diameter watch face—24k gold plating—quartz movement—red or black leather strap—leather gift box—"Credit Card Exclusive"—Disney Store Credit Card—$37.50.

Minnie Mouse (above left), Snow White (above) and Cinderella (left) quartz wristwatches for girls in plastic cases with vinyl bands. Issued by Lorus in 1987 and 1992-93.

1960s

A MICKEY MOUSE WATCH REVIVAL

The early 1960s saw few Mickey Mouse watches in the marketplace. One Mickey Mouse watch produced from 1960 to 1968, in fact, had no image, but simply the name "Mickey Mouse" printed below the numeral 12. A figurine of Mickey Mouse or Minnie Mouse in plastic or porcelain came as part of the package.

Illustrating the scarcity of Mickey Mouse watches in the 1960s is the following account from a Herb Caen column in the *San Francisco Chronicle*, Wednesday, July 21, 1965.

> Sententious thought for today: Little boys never grow up. They just become bigger little boys. Case in point:
>
> When Jim Killion of Atherton was 10 years old, his father (George Killion, President of American President Lines) promised him a Mickey Mouse watch and didn't come through—an oversight that Jim has never forgotten or forgiven. So the other day, Father George decided to make good, but wot & ho: the wonderful

One-of-a-kind "Love-In" Mickey Mouse–Minnie Mouse pocket watch. This beautiful and unique timepiece was originally designed by Pennsylvania antiques dealer and artist Al Horen of Renninger's Antique Market as a production model in the 1960s for the nostalgia marketplace.

Mickey Mousers of yesteryear, with the white-gloved hands and arms to indicate the time, are no longer on the market: Result: He is having one made by Sid Mobell, the Geary Street jeweler, on an Accutron body, with a price tag of $450 (Sid is copying the design from an original Mickey Mouse watch preserved under glass at the Planetarium in Golden Gate Park).

Jim Killion, now a killionare in his own right, is just about the happiest 40-year-old boy in town.

Long-haired hippies in tie-dyed T-shirts, hip-hugging bell-bottoms (or long flowing Indian print skirts) and sandals began sporting vintage 1930s Mickey Mouse watches they bought at flea markets and specialty antique jewelry stores. The original rodent-like, impish, white-faced, pie-eyed, long snout Mickey (as opposed to the late 1940s and 1950s

In the manner of R. Crumb, quintessential cartoonist for the hippie generation, John S. Fawcett created "Works of Art" comics featuring a pen and ink illustration of the Mickey Mouse watch.

pink flesh-faced version) was preferred by the Beat Generation. In the early to mid-sixties a Mickey Mouse watch was seldom seen; but by the late 1960s it became the fashion to wear one. Joe Cino, known as the father of the off-off Broadway theater movement, introduced the one-act plays he presented in his coffee-house theater—The Caffé Cino, on Cornelia Street in Greenwich Village—wearing a cape made from an American flag and his Ingersoll Mickey watch. The playwright Sam Shepard, whose work was presented at The Cino, also wore a Mickey Mouse watch in the late 1960s.

The Plastic Inevitable*

LEFT: *Orange vinyl Mickey Mouse toy wristwatch
with zipper compartment for coins or other stashables.*

RIGHT: *Yellow vinyl and red plastic children's playtime
Mickey Mouse wristwatch from Louis Marx & Co., marked
"Marx Toys" and "Walt Disney Productions."*

Plastic Wake to Music GE Mickey Mouse alarm clock/radio.
(TOP LEFT) Illco animated pre-school musical toy clock. Both
marked "Walt Disney Productions." (RIGHT) Playskool Mickey doll.

***The term "Plastic Inevitable" was coined by pop artist Andy Warhol in the 1960s
to signify the full-scale beginnings of the populuxe plastic age.**

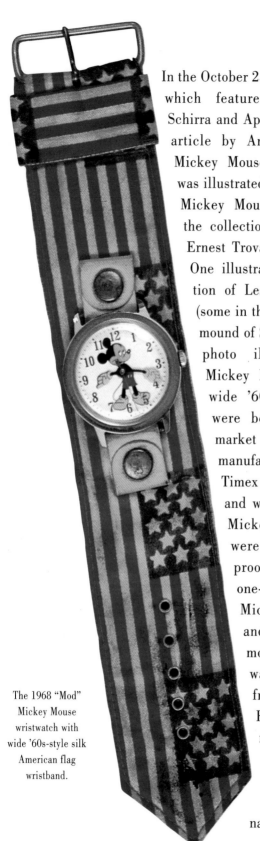

The 1968 "Mod" Mickey Mouse wristwatch with wide '60s-style silk American flag wristband.

In the October 25, 1968 *Life* magazine, which featured Astronaut Wally Schirra and Apollo 7 on its cover, an article by Ann Bayor celebrated Mickey Mouse's 40th birthday. It was illustrated with photos of 1930s Mickey Mouse memorabilia from the collections of Mel Birnkrant, Ernest Trova, and Robert Lesser. One illustration shows a collection of Lesser's 1930s watches (some in the original boxes) on a mound of Swiss cheese. Another photo illustrates the new Mickey Mouse watches (with wide '60s-style straps) that were being offered on the market in 1968. These were manufactured for adults by Timex (U.S. Time) at $12.95 and were called the "Mod" Mickey watches. They were waterproof, shock-proof and came with a one-year warranty. "Mod" Mickey had an orange and sometimes a pink mouse face; and the watch was a sellout from 1968 to 1971. Featuring the first newly designed image of Mickey since 1960, and including the Ingersoll brand name, the 1968 models were offered for Mickey's

40th birthday with a figurine. According to collector Hy Brown, it is the 1968 "Mod" Mickey watch that started the nostalgia craze that swept the country.

The *Life* magazine article states:

Mickey wristwatches are appearing on the wrists of models, movie stars and nostalgic, aging children of the Depression. Evidence of the way they are catching on came the other day when the Horn & Hardart chain of Automats, never especially noted for its awareness of fashion trends, offered as a "rodent-fetish special" a free slice of cheesecake to anyone wearing one.

Soon celebrities took to wearing either an original 1930s or a new 1960s watch, and they included Carol Burnett, TV host Johnny Carson, Tiny Tim, Grace Kelly, Andy Warhol, Ethel Kennedy, Sammy Davis, Jr., John Lennon, Truman Capote and Liberace. The June 1968 *Vogue* featured the Mickey Mouse Timex watch as worn by Lauren Hutton. Handsome Navy football captain Bill Dow of McLean, Virginia was pictured in the November 30, 1967 *Los Angeles Examiner* wearing a Mickey Mouse wristwatch which was traditionally worn by each Middie Captain prior to an Army game for good luck on the field.

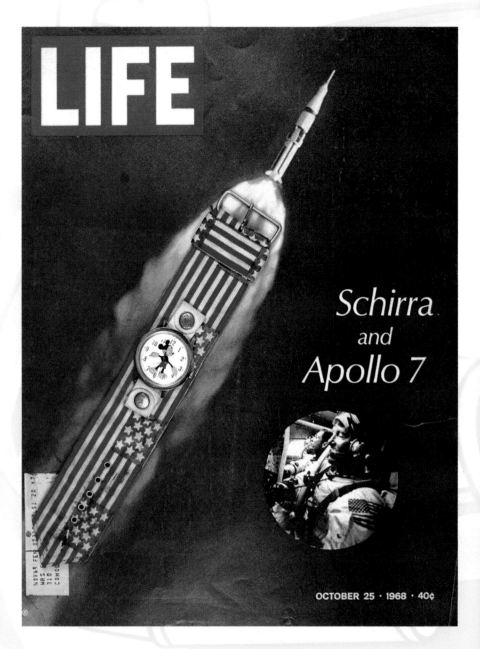

LIFE

Schirra
and
Apollo 7

OCTOBER 25 · 1968 · 40¢

MICKEY TO THE MOON

The big news came when Astronaut Wally
Schirra (born 1923) wore a Mickey Mouse
watch as a symbol of America in 1968 aboard
the Apollo 7 spacecraft that orbited the Earth.

Following this, the February 12, 1969 *Navy
Times* reported that Vice Admiral Bernard M.

Stream, chief of Naval Air Training, purchased a Mickey Mouse wristwatch at Disneyland which he gave to Commander Bill Wheat, officer in charge of the Blue Angels at the Naval Air station in Pensacola, Florida, who in turn presented it to Astronaut Commander Gene Cernan, who decided to wear his "honest to goodness Mickey Mouse ticker" on his trip to the moon on Apollo 10. The article in the *Navy Times* by John Hicks notes that:

> Aside from the humorous aspects of Navy officers wearing Mickey Mouse watches as they go about their serious business, it also is a tribute to the late Walt Disney, famed cartoonist who created Mickey and his sidekicks. Disney devoted part of his dreaming to the future. In Tomorrowland at Disneyland, there is a simulated trip to the moon, and now Cernan will be making the trip for real, making this part of Tomorrowland part of the present. And little Mickey Mouse, who recently celebrated his 40th birthday, will be riding with him.

Neiman Marcus Department Store responded to all of this outer space hoopla with a down-to-earth ad for its Men's Store in the *Dallas Morning News*, April 10, 1969. The ad pictures the old impish Mickey Mouse himself showing off his own 17 jewel Mickey Mouse wristwatch with the banner declaration borrowed from a Packard automobile advertising slogan: "Ask the Man Who Owns One."

"Mod" Mickey wristwatch with leather band.

1960−1968   Round dial, only the words "Mickey Mouse" below the numeral 12. No image of Mickey. A series made by U.S. Time included Mickey, Donald Duck, Alice in Wonderland, Cinderella and Snow White. The series all had red hands and red numerals and came with figurines in plastic or porcelain.

1966   Unauthorized version of the Mickey Mouse watch has Mickey with his tongue sticking out. The watch says "Swiss Made" but is otherwise unidentified.

1967−1969   Made in Japan by Seiko, 1" diameter round dial which has Mickey holding a hat.

1967−1969   Hamilton (Vantage), made in Japan, 1" diameter round dial has a modernized image of Mickey wearing red pants, yellow shoes and buttons. Sweep second hand with arrows. Labeled "Disneyland" above the image of Mickey and "Walt Disney Productions" below. These $19.95 watches, which came with black fabric bands, were sold only at the theme parks and as sendaways. There were three versions:

A) The first 500 watches manufactured had Mickey wearing white gloves, and have become rare collector's items. Later models came with red gloves.

B) A model with a clear plastic back to reveal works.

C) Electric, 17 jewels, resistant to shock, dust and magnetism. The second hand features a lightning bolt. The electric sold for $70.

1968—1971 U.S. Time's (Timex) first newly designed Mickey Mouse wristwatch since 1960 had a 1" round dial with black numbers. The numeral 5 appeared atop Mickey's left foot. Early versions had "Ingersoll © WDP" on the watch face to commemorate Mickey's 40th birthday. Later "Ingersoll" was dropped and "© WDP" appeared beneath the numeral 8. A model with a 3/4" dial was also offered and in 1971 an electric model with a sweep second hand. The watches were waterproof, shockproof, and carried a one-year guarantee. Many were packaged in a box with a figurine of Mickey. They came with wide leather or vinyl straps in a variety of styles for the Pop Age including bright red, light pink and black and white checks; there was also a snakeskin strap available to appeal to the counter-culture group. The "Mod" Mickey watches, as they are called by collectors, sold for $12.95. The small ones were $7.95. The electric Timex sold for $25.

1969—1971 The word "Disneyland" appears in several models above the figure of Mickey. 1" and 3/4" round dial models featured 17 jewel movement. Windert manufactured for sale at Disneyland.

"Mod" Minnie wristwatch with leather band.

1970s

THE NOSTALGIA DECADE

The 1970s invited everyone to walk down memory lane along with Kate Smith, Alice Faye, Ruby Keeler, Dick Powell, Ginger Rogers, and Fred Astaire and other newfound "old-timers"—and Mickey Mouse watches, new and old, came along for the ride. About the nostalgia fever that was beginning to sweep the country John Culhane stated in an article in the December 28, 1970 "Nostalgia Issue" of *Newsweek* magazine:

> Mickey Mouse watches are alive and ticking again—and will be exchanged as gifts this Christmas by the memory-haunted members of an age group that shunned them as "babyish" when they first appeared during the Depression. Mickey got a whole new lease on life in 1967 when Hippies wore watches to poke fun at the establishment. To everyone's amazement sales tripled in three years. In the past six months of 1970 alone, Mickey Mouse watches and clocks have brought in $7.5 million.

OPPOSITE: Esquire magazine, January 1971 issue, "Dubious Achievements of 1970!" featuring an original 1930s Mickey Mouse wristwatch on the cover.

A MICKEY MOUSE-EUM

In 1973, L. Bamberger's Department Store
in Newark, New Jersey created a special
Christmas Mouse-eum filled with a vast assort-
ment of more than 500 pieces of choice
Disneyana from the collection of Mel Birnkrant.
A leading Disneyana collector, Birnkrant owns
all of the pre-war original Ingersoll Mickey
Mouse timepieces, still in their original boxes.

Just inside the Mouse-eum entrance on the
fifth floor was a giant glowing red and blue neon
Mickey Mouse clock in which Mickey did a

somersault around the clock every minute, while his big gloved hands pointed to the hour and minute. The exhibits of memorabilia were encased in lighted plexiglas display boxes that were recessed into pre-fab wall units. One glittering box featured a display of Mickey Mouse watches and clocks. The exhibit celebrated Mickey Mouse's 45th birthday and attracted parents, children and collectors eager to get a look at Birnkrant's extensive collection.

The Emperor and Mickey Mouse

Following a tour of Disneyland in 1975, Emperor Hirohito of Japan was presented with a treasured memento—a Mickey Mouse wristwatch. The Emperor rarely took his Mickey watch off his wrist even at formal ceremonies. *People* magazine reported in its September 18, 1978 issue that the Royal Household was in dismay when the trusted Mickey watch stopped ticking. Concerned palace chamberlains took the watch to Tokyo experts who specialized in American timepieces. The diagnosis was that a new battery was required. When it was noted by all concerned that Mickey's hands once again were working, the watch was returned to the delighted Hirohito.

The Elgin Mickey

In the 1970s, retro-style Mickey Mouse watches were put forth to satisfy the nostalgia craze for the old-style 1930s Mickey with his pie-eyes, white face, and long snout. It was reported in the *Los Angeles Times* (July 21, 1971) that Elgin National Industries, Inc. and Disney signed a five-year watch and clock contract that went into effect January 1, 1972. Elgin would produce and distribute worldwide and would be the official manufacturer of timepieces to be sold at Walt Disney World in Florida, and Elgin's various brand-name timepieces would also be for sale at Disneyland in Anaheim. Bradley Time Division of Elgin National Industries produced most of the Disney character watches. Elgin/Bradley watches sold in the 1970s from $6.95 to $100.

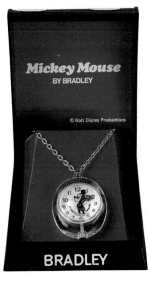

*Mickey Mouse Pendant-
Necklace watch made by
Bradley in 1972.*

1971 Mickey Mouse Electric—
"© WDP"—water resistant—black plastic
box—$25—Timex.

1972 Mickey Mouse Pendant—
Swiss made—necklace watch—1 1/8"—
"WDP"—Bradley.

1972 17 jewel round wristwatch with
standing figure of Mickey pointing to the
numerals with big-gloved hands—Helbros.

1972 The first of Elgin's
three Mickey Mouse electrics.

1972 Day/Date Calendar Watch—17 jewels—
unbreakable mainspring—water resistant—West
Germany—"WDP"—$50—Helbros.

1973 50th anniversary (1923–1973) of the
founding of The Walt Disney Company—
"50 Happy Years With Mickey" and
"Bradley Commemorative Series" on
back—Mickey's ears point to the
numeral 12 on dial—Bradley.

*Disney 50th Anniversary
Mickey Mouse watch—
Celebrating 50 Years of
the Walt Disney Studio—
1923-1973.*

1973 Mickey Mouse
Digital—1 1/16" x 1/2" rectangular—$19.95—Bradley.

*Mickey Mouse pocket
watch made in Great
Britain, 1973.*

1975 Mickey Mouse Club—
1" round—Mickey Mouse
Club Logo—"W. D. P."
and "MOUSEKETEER"—
$15.95—Bradley.

*"Mouseketeer" wristwatch
issued for the 1975 Mickey
Mouse Club revival on T.V.*

Minuteman Mickey

Litho on cardboard die-cut display sign from Walt Disney World, 1976.

AMERICA ON PARADE

A Star-Spangled Extravaganza Featuring ...
200 Years of History in Motion:
Disney-Style
June 7, 1975 thru September 6, 1976

Walt Disney World

Mickey Mouse Official Bicentennial watch in original box.

Mickey Mouse Bulova Accutron sold in 1976 for $150.

1975 Bicentennial Mickey Mouse—1 ⅛" round image of Mickey clad in Revolutionary War uniform—"July 4, 1776"—$15.95—Bradley.

1975 Mickey Mouse—oval ¾"—"© WDP"—$16.95—Bradley.

1975 Mickey Mouse and Goofy—Bradley.

1976 Mickey Mouse Bulova Accutron—Round dial on rectangular casing—day/date calendar—water resistant—stainless steel—high-pitched tone emanates from watch alternately—$150.

1978 "Moving Head" Mickey Mouse wristwatch—companion piece, "Moving Head" Minnie Mouse—$18.95—Bradley.

Mickey in 1776 outfit on
Mickey Mouse Bicentennial
wristwatch.

Bicentennial Mickey
Mouse pocket watch.

1978 Bradley "Sports" watches—Mickey Mouse plays
baseball, football, tennis, basketball—$15.95.

1978 Mickey's 50th Birthday—"Registered
Commemorative Edition"—Happy Birthday logo
with Mickey Mouse silhouette—round or rectangular model with gold casing featuring the old style
1930s Mickey
Mouse with
white face and
pie-eyes—
Mickey's ears
point to the
numeral 11—$18.95
(rect. $19.95)—Bradley.

Mickey Mouse
wristwatch,
Bradley, 1973.

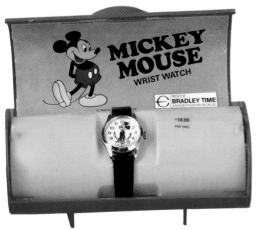

Mickey Mouse wristwatch in
plastic box, Bradley, 1973.

1978 "Skin-diver" Mickey—1" round black case with black strap—date window—waterproof—$21.95—Bradley.

1979 "Disco Mickey"—black watch face with "disco lite" colored circles—Mickey on dance floor in John Travolta suit—packaged with a special "Disco Mouse" record—$19.95—Bradley.

"Skin Diver" Mickey Mouse waterproof wristwatch, 1978.

Disco Mickey

Mickey Mouse on the cover of Life *magazine Disco issue, November 1978.*

ABOVE: *Original "Disco Mickey" wristwatch box featuring Mickey in his white, bell-bottomed John Travolta* Saturday Night Fever *outfit.*

LEFT: *"Disco Mickey" wristwatch, 1979.*

BELOW: *Buena Vista Records 45 rpm recording of "Disco Mouse" performed by the Mouseketeers was a bonus offered with the "Disco Mickey" wristwatch.*

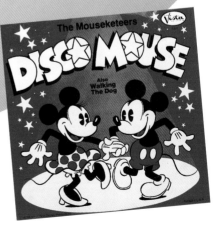

1980s–1990s

A Classic Collectibles Boom

As America and the world looked ahead to the approaching millennium in the 1980s and 1990s, one eye was kept clearly focused on the past images of the 20th century. The important modernist World's Fair of 1933–34 in Chicago, the New York and California World's Fairs of 1939–40 and the New York World's Fair of 1964–65 all looked forward to the new techno-logical future—"The World of Tomorrow." A time of ease, comfort and plenitude that the Fairs promised was just around the corner. In many instances today, the dreams and experiments that were first seen at the World's Fairs have become realities.

By the 1980s and 1990s writers, historians and collectors have dug into the "old" century with the determination of archeologists in search of what is relevant in terms of popular culture and mass production. For one, collecting Disney mem-orabilia, once considered to be just a nostalgic good fun hobby, was by the '80s being taken more

OPPOSITE:
Mickey Mouse musical alarm wrist-watch with "Flags of all Nations" as watch numerals—Lorus Quartz.

The Mickey Mouse—Minnie Mouse pocket watch originally designed in the 1960s by Al Horen was offered as a free gift to Disney Store Limited Edition Watch Collector's Club members who purchased the complete Series V collection of six Disney character wristwatches which included Snow White and the Seven Dwarfs, the Little Mermaid and Pocahontas. 1996 sales brochure.

seriously. Labeled "Classic Collectibles" or simply "Classic," some of the artifacts jumped unexpectedly sky-high in the antiques or Disneyana marketplaces, particularly those items from the "Golden Age" of the 1920s, 1930s, and 1940s and from what is now regarded as the "Silver Age"—the 1950s and 1960s. Avid collectors and museum archivists have created categories such as artwork, toys and watches and advised shoppers what to look for at antique shows, flea markets and in stores.

By the 1980s all the important international auction houses—including Christie's, Sotheby's and Phillips—developed adjunct "collectible" departments, many of which handled specific Mickey Mouse memorabilia like toys and character watches. An auction on October 5, 1981 held by Phillips Son & Neal, Inc. sold an Ingersoll U.S. Time Mickey Mouse wristwatch for $120. With a diminishing number of bona-fide collectibles to be found from the "Golden" or "Silver Age" decades and with prices soaring at big collectible extravaganzas, manufacturers came into the picture in the 1980s and 1990s to produce what are called "instant collectibles" or "investibles."

In the arena of Mickey Mouse watches and Disney timepieces these "wearables" and ticking clocks that turn up in Disney Stores, department stores, jewelry stores, specialty shops and in mail-order catalogs have a limited production, making them more desirable as collector's items. In 1986 the Seiko Watch

Company with its subsidiary company Lorus was awarded the license for Disney character watches. Various other companies were also given rights to produce watches exclusively for the Disney theme parks or for Disney employees. The Seiko/Lorus Disney watch business is still going strong. Seiko, Elgin and others in the 1980s and 1990s produced Limited Editions in limited quantities, making them instant collectibles in the active watch marketplace. A great many varieties exist, and many are exceptional in terms of concept and design.

In the 1980s and 1990s Mickey Mouse remained King of the Watch—designed to capture his original 1930s glory. The vintage look for the Mickey of the Depression era was a top seller in the 1980s and into the decade of the 1990s.

The Disney Stores across the country and the Disney theme parks in California, Florida, Tokyo and Paris have played a big part in promoting the Mickey Mouse watch (and other Disney characters on timepieces) and the variety and sheer volume of these is astounding.

The Disney Store front on 42nd Street in New York City.

Ladies' & Gents' Lorus Pair

Lorus quartz watches designed after the original Ingersoll 1930s Mickey Mouse watch, 1988. Ladies' watch (left). Men's watch (right).

1980 Mickey and Minnie Disco—1" round, black watch face—Minnie in red dress—Mickey in blue suit—animated heads—rotating outer ring—flashing lights illusion—Bradley.

1980 Disneyland 25th Anniversary—Elgin.

1980 Digital Quartz—made in Japan—blinking, animated eyes on round TV screen—Alba—K Hattori & Co., Ltd.

1980 Square and oval Mickey Mouse silver bangle watches—Bradley.

1981 Mickey gold figure in relief—17 jewels, stars for numerals—Bradley—$27.00.

1981 Series of four by Alba—$35 to $40 each—all digital.

1) William Tell Mickey alarm wristwatch— Mickey shoots arrows at falling apples, digital game.

2) Mickey and Minnie musical alarm—plays theme from "Mickey Mouse Club"— Minnie's eyes wink.

3) Mickey and Minnie "Valentine" musical alarm— Mickey throws kisses to Minnie—plays "Holidays" and "Cuckoo Waltz."

4) Mickey and Minnie Tennis, musical alarm and game—plays "Jambalaya" and "De Camptown Race."

1982 Mickey Mouse LCD—Quartz— 7/8" dial—Bradley.

1982 Cowboy Mickey—Mickey is twirling a lariat— 1" face—western tooled leather band—$23—Bradley.

LEFT AND BELOW: *"Cowboy Mickey" with Western tooled leather strap and buckle, Bradley, 1982.*

*1983 celebrated the 50th Anniversary
of the Mickey Mouse wristwatch.
"Happy Birthday Mickey"
Commemorative Watch ad from Bradley Time
(above). Walt Disney Commemorative Official Mickey Mouse wristwatch in
original box, "50 Happy Years," Limited Edition, Bradley (above right).*

1982 Mickey and Pluto LCD—Quartz—1" face—also
a model with standard movement with a 7/8" face—Mickey
is holding a bone—Pluto has a wagging head—
$21/$25—Bradley.

1983 50th Anniversary of the Mickey Mouse Watch—
1933–1983—7/8" face—gold case—leather band—quartz in
men's and women's styles—inscribed on back: "50 Years of
Time with Mickey" and "Registered Limited Edition"—Mickey's
ears point to the numeral 1 (a reference to the first Bradley
commemorative of 1973)—with or without calendars—Bradley.

1983   Mickey Mouse Auto Racer—black acrylic case—with tachymeter—Bradley.

1984   Mickey as Sorcerer's Apprentice— made in Hong Kong—digital with day/date— Disney Channel Premium.

1984   Mickey Runner—pop-up LCD—square red plastic case—1 1/8" face—red plastic band—figure of Mickey against yellow circle background— pop-up button on face—Bradley.

"Sorcerer's Apprentice" Mickey Mouse digital wristwatch, 1984.

1984   14k Gold Mickey Mouse—Mickey head from cartoon opening— 1 1/8" face—gold mesh band—Men's: $3,500/Ladies': $1,800— Baume & Mercier, Geneva.

1984   Donald Duck 50th Birthday— digital quartz—1" blue face—Donald Duck Birthday logo—black strap—blister-pack package—$4.25 offer—from Donald Duck Orange Juice promotion.

Lorus Quartz Donald Duck wristwatch.

1984   Donald Duck 50th Birthday—round face— inscribed on back: "Birthday Commemorative Edition— Donald Duck, Registered"— plastic band— $28—Bradley.

Donald Duck "Happy Birthday" wristwatch in the original box, 1984.

1985 Disney Summer Magic—Mickey against NYC skyline—$4.95—Produced by Lorus for Walt Disney Specialty Products.

1985 30th Anniversary of Disneyland—Mouse ears and banner—men's and ladies' giveaways—two other styles were also offered by Bradley.

Disney Summer Magic 1985 Mickey Mouse digital wristwatch.

1988 Mickey Mouse 60th Birthday—Sun Coast Manufacturers—round face—digital— "Mickey/Disneyland—1988—The Walt Disney Company—Made in China" on back.

1988 Mickey's 60th Birthday—"60 Years with You" Mickey celebration—quartz—second hand with three Mickeys with arrow pointing to slash marks indicating the seconds—men's and ladies'—$54.95—Lorus.

1988 Lorus Quartz wristwatch is a modified reproduction of Mickey Number One.

Mickey at Sixty

RIGHT: *1988 Seiko Collection wristwatch models for Mickey's 60th Birthday. Inscribed on the reverse is "Mickey Mouse Since 1928."*

LEFT: *Seiko 60th Birthday watch with box. The watch is a modified reproduction of original with single Mickey running around the second hand.*

1988 Mickey's 60th Birthday—"Seiko Collection"—quartz with rectangular case—second hand with *one* running Mickey—inscription on back "Mickey Mouse Since 1928"—red plastic box in red, white and black cardboard package with figures of Mickey—men's or ladies'—$195 with leather strap—$225 with expanding band.

1989 Tokyo Disneyland—"American Oldies"—Mickey and Minnie with classic 1950s automobile—Tokyo Disneyland also offered a commemorative wristwatch and pin for the opening day of "Star Tours," July 12, 1989. The crystal of the watch has hologram Star Tours scene.

1988 Huey, Dewey, and Louie—quartz—wristwatch from Disney's *Ducktales*—"The Walt Disney Company" on back—Lorus.

1988 Mickey Mouse Club—neon logo distributed as part of the Mickey Mouse club Membership Kit for subscriber/members.

First wristwatch featuring both Mickey and Donald, 1989, Lorus.

1989 Mickey and Donald—quartz—characters in ³/4-length view—Lorus.

1989 Cameraman Mickey Mouse—silhouette in black—Lorus—quartz.

REPRO MICKEY

Reproduction of original Ingersoll 1933 Mickey Number One featuring three-Mickey second hand and metal link band with die-cut metal Mickeys, Pedre, 1990.

Pedre reproduction of original 1933 box, 1990.

1990 Pedre—reproduction of original Ingersoll 1933 Mickey Number One—1 1/8" round watch face—Three-Mickey second hand—"Mickey Mouse Pedre" on dial—Mickey cut-out link wristband—packaged in reproduction of original 1933 orange box— Limited Edition of 25,000—$90—Note: In 1991 Pedre offered the same watch with the Mickey cut-outs on a leather wristband in a reproduction of the 1930s blue cardboard hinged box with a four-color illustration of Mickey on top.

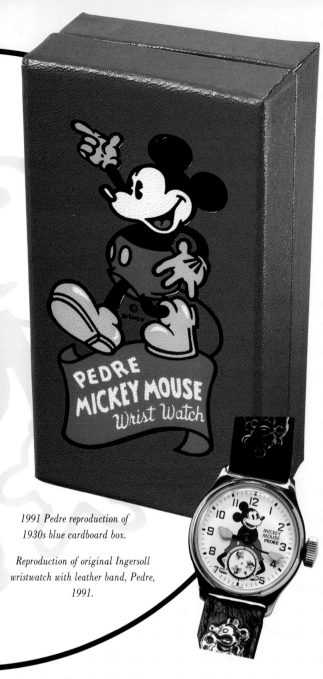

1991 Pedre reproduction of 1930s blue cardboard box.

Reproduction of original Ingersoll wristwatch with leather band, Pedre, 1991.

1990 Mick Tracy—Mickey as Dick with yellow detective hat on watch face with primary ***Dick Tracy*** movie logo colors—Limited Edition of 3,000 for Cast Member Summer picnic— Ballanda Corporation.

LEFT AND RIGHT: *Mick Tracy wristwatch inspired by the Dick Tracy movie starring Warren Beatty and Madonna.*

1990 Mickey Astaire—Mickey in tuxedo and top hat— $89.50—Pedre.

1990 Mickey Mouse "Talking Time"—$29.98—Sounds Fun, Inc.

1991 20th Anniversary of Walt Disney World —"20 Magical Years"—white watch face with yellow, magenta and teal logo design—$49.95—Lorus Seiko.

1991 1930s Mickey Mouse— Limited Series—handmade 18k gold with mother-of-pearl dial to commemorate 36 years of Disney Magic—$15,500.

Mickey "Astaire" wristwatch, after Fred Astaire.

1992 20th Anniversary of Walt Disney World—made for cast members through Company D at Walt Disney World—Sweda.

1992 Mickey Mouse—at Euro Disneyland Castle—***Disney News*** magazine/Ballanda.

1992 65th Mickey Mouse Birthday—Limited Edition of 5,000—metal case—Overseas Products International.

Diamond studded Minnie Mouse "Marilyn Monroe" wristwatch after The Seven Year Itch, was issued as a companion piece to Mickey "Astaire."

1992   Classic old-style Mickey Mouse—inscription on back "Made Exclusively for The Disney Store"—$55—Fossil.

1992   Mickey and Pluto—depicts Mickey chasing Pluto on clear circular disc—"Made Exclusively for The Disney Store" packaged in metal tin—Fossil.

1992   Mickey Mouse—at first Disneyana Convention—Limited Edition of 1,500—Overseas products International—$75.

1992   Mickey Mouse with monthly calendar and date—exclusive to the Disney Store—$75—Advance Watch Company.

1993   "Mickey's Workshop"—Japanese—Christmas musical watch features Mickey in a Santa costume and Pluto with the caption "1993 Seasons Greetings"—plays medley of Christmas songs—Limited Edition of 2,000—exclusive to Disney Theme Parks and Resorts.

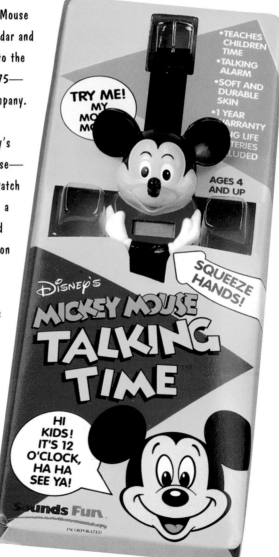

"Talking Time" Mickey Mouse wristwatch in original box.

1994   Donald Duck 60th Birthday—reproduction of the original 1935 Donald Duck wristwatch—Round, 1 1/8" watch face reads "Donald Duck Pedre"—Donald in a sailor suit points to the time with feathered hands—second hand disc features three tiny Donald Ducks—Donald Duck enamel cut-outs adorn black leather band—packaged in a replica of the original box—$75—Pedre—with The Disney Store.

1994   Donald Duck 60th Birthday—modified reproduction of original 1936 Ingersoll Donald Duck wristwatch—second hand with three tiny Mickeys—Limited edition of 5,000—$65—Timex.

OTHER 1990s WATCHES

Steamboat Willie—Mickey Mouse wristwatch—packaged in a "book" in limited edition of 7,500—Walt Disney Classic Limited Edition Series II—$70.

Mickey Mouse as a nutcracker for Christmas—made exclusively for The Disney Store—packaged in a metal tin.

Mickey Mouse chronograph—limited edition of 5,000—made exclusively for Walt Disney Theme Parks and Resorts—packaged in a metal tin—$145.

Walt Disney—famous pose of Walt with Mickey's shadow—limited edition of 5,000—made exclusively for Walt Disney Theme Parks and Resorts—$75.

Disney Synergy—Mickey Mouse design—produced for internal use by the Corporate Synergy Department of Walt Disney Studio.

Disney Synergy wristwatch.

New-Old Mickey Pocket Watches

1996–1997 Colibri Collection

Colibri has manufactured stunning Mickey Mouse pocket watches for Mickey & Co., some with 17 jewel movements and fobs. In gold or silver, the watches feature the original 1930s style Mickey, a "Railroad" Mickey, and *Steamboat Willie* Mickey.

Fossil Watches

Mickey Mouse Fossil watch with wooden toy "train"—a replica of the 1940s Fisher-Price toys. (Note: The Fossil watch boxes are marked "Adult Collector's Item: Not Intended for use by Children.")

Mickey Mouse watch with wooden "Mickey Drummer" pull-toy, 1996–1997—limited to 15,000 ($80).

Fossil puts forth any number of splendid comic characters on watches including Felix the Cat and legendary cowboy Roy Rogers, cowgirl Dale Evans and The Lone Ranger. They are noted for a selection of limited edition classic Mickey Mouse watches that are among the best designed Mickey timepieces produced in the marketplace today. Specialty watches like the ones

Disney Store front at 42nd Street and 7th Avenue in New York City features an outsized industrial-style Mickey Mouse clock from Fossil, after a watch made just for this particular store.

issued in 1997 for sale just at The Disney Store on 42nd Street in New York, have become the "must-have" instant collectible watches of

Mickey pocket watch with glazed ceramic figurine, Fossil.

the 1990s. On this one a classic Mickey image stands atop the Fossil logo—reminiscent but not an exact copy of the original Ingersoll. The watch is a repeat of the outsized clock on the outside of the 42nd Street Disney Store.

Fossil Mickey Mouse Limited Edition Pocket Watch box.

MICKEY MOUSE MILLENNIUM

M ickey Mouse will be 70 years old on November 18, 1998. Yet we continue to think of Mickey as a sprite who is forever young. In the year 2003 pop-culture-guru-icon Mickey will be 75; and in 2028 he celebrates his very own centennial. Mickey Mouse at 75 and at 100 in the new century is a thought to contemplate.

Will we be looking at a Mickey image on a wristwatch, pocket watch, or clock in the 21st century? Of this there is little doubt; and certainly there will be commemorative watches for each of these important dates.

Mickey Mouse himself has become timeless; and surely he will always remain on the job as a very special Father Time. The sense of continuity and the plain good fun Mickey brings to time seems to alleviate the weight of minutes, hours, days, weeks, months, years, decades, and centuries.

And so we elect Mickey Mouse our "official" perennial timekeeper. When examining the hour and minute in a day, we must have M-I-C-K-E-Y M-O-U-S-E!

OPPOSITE:
Six-ounce paper party cup featuring Mickey Mouse on a "Happy Birthday" rocket ship heading into outer space. Produced in the 1960s by Beach Product, Inc. of Kalamazoo, Michigan and marked "Walt Disney Productions."

INDEX

SELECTED BIBLIOGRAPHY

Bain, David, and Bruce Harris, eds. *Mickey Mouse—Fifty Happy Years.* New York: Harmony Books, 1978.

Brenner, Howard S., *Comic Character Clocks and Watches.* Florence, ALA: Books Americana, Inc., 1987.

Brown, Hy, with Nancy Thomas. *Comic Character Timepieces.* Philadelphia: Schiffer Publishing, Ltd., 1992.

Culhane, John. *Walt Disney's Fantasia.* New York: Harry N. Abrams, 1983.

Feild, Robert D. *The Art of Walt Disney.* London: William Collins, 1947.

Hake, Ted. *Hake's Guide to TV Collectibles.* Radnor, PA: Wallace-Homestead Book Co., 1990.

Heide, Robert, and John Gilman. *Disneyana—Classic Collectibles 1928–1958.* New York: Hyperion, 1994.

Heide, Robert, and John Gilman. *Cartoon Collectibles—50 Years of Dime-Store Memorabilia.* New York: Doubleday, 1983.

Hine, Thomas. *Populuxe.* New York: Alfred A. Knopf, 1986.

Lesser, Robert. *A Celebration of Comic Art and Memorabilia.* New York: Hawthorn Books, 1975.

Maltin, Leonard. *The Disney Films—3rd Edition.* New York: Hyperion, 1995.

Merritt, Russell, and J. B. Kaufman. *Walt in Wonderland.* Baltimore: Johns Hopkins University Press, 1993.

Morra-Yoe, Janet, and Craig Yoe. *The Art of Mickey Mouse.* New York: Hyperion, 1991.

Munsey, Cecil. *Disneyana.* New York: Hawthorn Books, 1974.

Phillips, Cabell. *From the Crash to the Blitz—1929–1939—The New York Times Chronicle of American Life.* New York: Macmillan, 1969.

Shine, Bernard C., Principal Consultant. *Mickey Mouse Memorabilia—Vintage Years 1928– 1938.* New York: Harry N. Abrams, 1986.

Smith, Dave. *Disney A to Z.* New York: Hyperion, 1996.

Tumbusch, Tom. *Tomart's Illustrated Disneyana Catalog & Price Guide.* Dayton, OH: Tomart Publications, 1989.

Unger, Stewart. *American Wristwatches—Five Decades of Style & Design.* Atglen, Philadelphia: Schiffer Publishing, Ltd., 1996.

ABOUT THE AUTHORS

ROBERT HEIDE was born and grew up in Irvington, New Jersey. He was educated at Northwestern University in Evanston, Illinois. He now lives in Manhattan. Called a seminal playwright of off-Broadway and off-off Broadway by the *Village Voice*, his best known works are *The Bed, Moon, At War with the Mongols, Suburban Tremens, American Hamburger*, and *Tropical Fever in Key West*. Andy Warhol filmed Heide's play *The Bed* (Warhol's first split screen) and he wrote the scenario for the Warhol film *Lupe* starring Edie Sedgwick. Heide also appeared in two Warhol films *Camp* and *Dracula/Sabbath*, both with Jack Smith.

JOHN GILMAN was born in Honolulu and he spent his youth in San Francisco and Grosse Pointe. He currently resides in Greenwich Village. Gilman has acted in and produced plays off-Broadway and off-off Broadway at the Caffe Cino, Cafe La Mama, Judson Church, Westbeth Theater Center, Theater for the New City, and recently appeared in the Tom O'Horgan–directed theatrical production of *Greed/Flood* at Here Theater in Soho. Formerly the executive director of the American Society of Magazine Photographers, he has contributed photographs to several publications, including the *Village Voice*, *The Daily News* and many of his books, including *The Mickey Mouse Watch*.

Profiled in articles in *The New York Times*, *The Daily News*, and other periodicals, the co-authors' television appearances include "The Today Show" with Katie Couric, "Entertainment Tonight" with Leonard Maltin, "The Tom Snyder Show," the Fox network, and other television and radio programs.

Authors John Gilman (left) and Robert Heide in front of the Unisphere (symbol of the 1964–65 New York World's Fair) in Flushing Meadow— Corona Park, Flushing, New York.

Robert Heide and John Gilman are the co-authors of the following books:

Disneyana: Classic Collectibles 1928–1958

Home Front America: Popular Culture of the World War II Era

Greenwich Village: A Primo Guide to Shopping, Eating, and Making Merry in True Bohemia

O' New Jersey: Daytripping, Back Roads, Eateries, and Funky Adventures

Popular Art Deco: Depression Era Style and Design

Box-Office Buckaroos: The Cowboy Hero from the Wild West Show to the Silver Screen

Starstruck: The Wonderful World of Movie Memorabilia

Cartoon Collectibles: 50 Years of Dime-Store Memorabilia

Cowboy Collectibles

Dime-Store Dream Parade: Popular Culture 1925–1955

ACKNOWLEDGMENTS

At Hyperion—special thanks to Wendy Lefkon and Bob Miller for their indomitable faith in this book project. Thanks also to Tracey George in Publicity and David Lott in Pre-production.

Thanks to Wendy Lipkind—authors' agent.

At Welcome Enterprises, Inc.—Sara Baysinger, Jon Glick, Hiro Clark Wakabayashi and Gregory Wakabayashi.

Thanks especially to Dave Smith, Director of the Disney Archives where we found our primary sources of watch information and were granted invaluable access to the greatest number of original watches. Thanks also to Robert Tieman, Rebecca Cline, Colette Espino and Adina Lerner at the Archives in Burbank.

At Disney Consumer Products—Joel Burnett, Aviva Gordon.

At Buena Vista Pictures—Mary Eileen O'Donnell.

Thanks to Philip Cohen Photographics (41 Yosemite Avenue, Oakland, CA 94611) who photographed watches and related memorabilia at the Disney Archives.

At Christie's East—Tim Luke, Vice President/toy specialist, Christie's Collectibles.

At Collector's Showcase Magazine, Dallas, Texas, Chey Reynolds, co-publisher.

At the King Company, Austin, Texas (exclusive distributors of Lorus and Jaz/Mickey & Co.)—Bob Kirch, Lisa Martin, Vince Lewis.

At Fossil—Merk Harbour. Fossil Watch Company has an official collector's club (write to: Fossil Collector's Club, 2280 N. Greenville Ave., Richardson, TX 75082).

At Colibri, Linden Clock Division, Providence, RI—Steve Trust, Product Manager, and Carol Lyons.

Some collectors such as Hy Brown, Stewart Unger, Howard Brenner and Tom Tumbusch have catalogued Mickey Mouse watches in collector volumes (see bibliography) and Disneyana periodicals; and Ted Hake has featured many of the Disney watches over the years in his auction catalogs (write to: Ted Hake's Americana, PO Box 1444, York, PA. 17405). Other specialist dealers and collectors like Bernard C. Shine, Tracy Terhune, Henry Mazzeo, Robert Lesser, George Hattersley, Doug and Pat Wengel, 'Tiques of Old Bridge, New Jersey, and Time Will Tell Unlimited, Inc. at 962 Madison Avenue, New York, were consulted in the early stages of the development of this book.

Thanks also to the following for their support: Callie Angell, Kenneth Anger, Robert Bryan, Jacque Lynn Colton, Rich Conaty, WQEW, John and Tracy Currie, Jim Fitzgerald, Steve Gould, Anne and George Harris (and family), Madeline Hoffer, Nancy Keller, Sally Kirkland, Paul Leiber, Mark Simon, Bill Stern, William Strauss, LiseBeth Talbot and Gwenn Victor.

For information address Hyperion, 114 Fifth Avenue, New York, NY, 10011

Produced by Welcome Enterprises, Inc., 588 Broadway, New York, NY 10012

Project Director: Sara Baysinger
Designer: Jon Glick
Hyperion Editor: Wendy Lefkon
Assistant Editor: Robin Friedman

ISBN: 0–7868–6343–9

Printed in Singapore by Toppan Printing Co., Inc.

FIRST EDITION

2 4 6 8 10 9 7 5 3 1